PRESENTED TO:

_____

FROM:

_____

DATE:

_____

LIVE
LEARN
LEAD

to Make a Difference

by

DON SODERQUIST

Published by J. Countryman® a division of Thomas Nelson, Inc.,
Nashville, Tennessee 37214

Contributing Writer: Mark Gilroy, of Mark Gilroy Communications, Inc. Tulsa, OK

www.jcountryman.com
www.thomasnelson.com

Designed by Greg Jackson, Thinkpen Design, llc

ISBN 1-4041-0149-7

Printed and bound in the United States of America

Table of Contents

Foreword

Live, Learn, and Lead

He has showed you, O man, what is good.

And what does the LORD require of you? To act justly

and to love mercy and to walk humbly with your God.

MICAH 6:8, NIV

This book is a small glimpse into a few of the life lessons I've picked up on my journey as a business leader, but much more importantly, as someone who loves God and has desired to live for Him in all areas of my life.

I don't hold myself up as a perfect example for you to follow, but my prayer is that something I have experienced and observed will impact you in a personal, positive, and powerful way.

Just as the prophet Micah keeps things simple by reminding us that what God looks for is men and women who will "act justly, love mercy and walk humbly with God," so the simple outline of this book serves notice that I'm not trying to break new ground, but to provide reminders and put emphasis on basic life issues that make a profound difference on how all of us can better live, learn, and lead.

Are you ready to live a more positive and joyful life—not in the shadows of unhappiness and small spiritedness, but in the sunlight of the marvelous gift of life you have received from God?

Are you ready to learn more from the experiences of life—not just facts and head knowledge, but about how to take steps to reach your full potential?

Are you ready to make your life count for something in the hearts and lives of others—to positively impact the lives of those who see you in action every day?

I hope your answer to all three questions is "yes," and that you will allow God to bless you as you live, learn, and lead in your corner of the world.

Don Soderquist

PART ONE
LIVE WITH PURPOSE

Not that I have already attained, or am already perfected;
but I press on, that I may lay hold of that
for which Christ Jesus has also laid hold of me.

PHILIPPIANS 3:12

When I was a young man, I wanted to change the world.
I found it was difficult to change the world, so I tried to
change my nation. When I found I couldn't change the
nation, I began to focus on my town. I couldn't change the
town and as an older man, I tried to change my family. Now,
as an old man, I realize the only thing I can change is myself,
and suddenly I realize that if long ago I had changed myself,
I could have made an impact on my family. My family and
I could have made an impact on our town. Their impact
could have changed the nation and I could
indeed have changed the world.

UNKNOWN MONK, A.D. 1100

Live with Purpose by ...

Recognizing Your Creator

For, after all, put it as we may to ourselves, we are all of us from birth to death guests at a table which we did not spread.   The sun, the earth, love, friends, our very breath are parts of the banquet. Shall we think of the day as a chance to come nearer to our Host, and to find out something of Him who has fed us so long?

REBECCA HARDING DAVIS

We've all known someone who takes all the credit for his success without acknowledging those who helped him—and blames others for everything that goes wrong.   We may not respect someone like that, but all of us are at least tempted to pat ourselves on the back in recognition of our many fine contributions when things turn out wonderful in life and quickly shift the blame to others—sometimes even to God—when things break down.

A wise person, a person who knows the secret to living a great life, understands that all good gifts are from God—that we would not even exist if not for God, much less be able to achieve anything great or small.

How wise are you when it comes to acknowledging God? Do you worship Him as Creator? Do you thank Him as Deliverer and Provider? Do you trust Him and His Will for your life—even when it doesn't make perfect sense to you—as the One who is all-knowing? Do you love Him as Your Heavenly Father? Do you talk to Him throughout the day as your Friend?

The writer of Proverbs says that "the fear of the Lord is the beginning of knowledge" (1:7). The word translated "fear" in most English Bible translations is actually reverence. How much respect do you show for God? In a culture that routinely uses God's name as an expletive rather than as part of worship, we would do well to evidence some healthy awe and "fear" of God in our lives.

I love the way author and gifted communicator Roy Lessin weaves together acknowledging God with discovering our true purpose in life:

> *Just think,*
> *You're not here by chance*
> *But by God's choosing.*
> *His hands formed you and*
> *Made you the person you are.*
> *He compares you to no one else—*
> *You are one of a kind.*
> *You lack nothing*
> *That His grace can't give you.*
> *He has allowed you to be here*
> *At this time in history*
> *To fulfill His special purpose.*

For this generation.
You are God's servant
In God's place
At God's perfect time.

If we could fully grasp those words and thoughts, I think it might change the way we live our lives and help us find a new sense of peace and purpose as we recognize our Creator.   If we accept the fact that our very lives are a gift from God, our natural response will be to honor Him in all we do.

For thus says the Lord, Who created the heavens,
Who is God, Who formed the earth and made it,
Who has established it, Who did not create it
in vain, Who formed it to be inhabited:
"I am the Lord, and there is no other."

ISAIAH 45:18

Live with Purpose by ...

Having Determination

The essence of optimism is that it takes no account of the present, but it is a source of inspiration, of vitality and hope where others have resigned; it enables a man to hold his head high, to claim the future for himself and not to abandon it to his enemy.

DIETRICH BONHOEFFER

Every one of us will encounter difficulties and setbacks in our lives. How do we handle them? Do we persevere? Do we bounce back and try again?

I was watching two of the participants at our experiential learning course that's part of the Center for Leadership and Ethics at John Brown University. Their particular assignment was to scale a fifty-foot alpine tower, no easy feat. Of course, everyone reacts differently if they fail to reach the top. Some just give up and accept the fact that they couldn't do it. Others try two, three, even four and five more times, determined to make it to the top. Many of them are able to get there on their second or third try, but even if they don't, they usually reach a higher mark than they did the first time and that they ever thought they could. Sure enough, the second person, probably a little out of shape, but very determined, grunted and groaned and reached the top on his third attempt.

Isn't that a perfect picture of what happens in life? And how different people respond?

Truly, the mark of an excellent person is not seen in their accomplishments, but in how they handle defeats. There are countless examples of great people who persevered, and the following may be one of the greatest:

In 1831, he failed in business.

In 1832, he was defeated for the state legislature.

In 1833, he failed in business again.

In 1834, he was elected to the state legislature.

In 1838, he was defeated for speaker.

In 1840, he was defeated for elector.

In 1843, he was defeated for U.S. Congress.

In 1855, he was defeated for the U.S. Senate.

In 1856, he was defeated for vice president of
the United States.

In 1858, he was defeated for the U.S. Senate.

In 1861, he was elected as the sixteenth
president of the United States.

Abraham Lincoln is widely recognized by historians as one of the greatest presidents in our nation's history. And what a model of determination he is to all of us who have struggled on the way to achieving a goal.

When I first heard the Wal-Mart story from beginning to end, I was surprised to learn that Sam had unexpectedly lost the lease on his first store. He didn't let a setback like losing his first building stop him. He quickly found a new store location and set up shop. It made me wonder, what if Sam had given up on owning his own store after he lost his lease? Because of hindsight, we may scoff at that thought, but giving up would be the much more common response. If Sam had given up, I believe the world would be a different place.

How do you respond to setbacks in life, whether at work or in your family or in your personal life? Do you shut down in the face of disappointment? Do you look for greener pastures? Or, do you dig a little deeper in your soul and find the strength to overcome? Be assured that no worthwhile endeavor will be without pain and disappointment.

Yet in all these things we are more than conquerors through Him who loved us.

ROMANS 8:37

Live with Purpose by ...

Expressing Gratitude

Thank God every morning when you get up that you have something to do that day which must be done, whether you like it or not. Being forced to work and forced to do your best will breed in you temperance and self-control, diligence and strength of will, cheerfulness and content, and a hundred virtues which the idle never know.

KINGSLEY

We've all seen children who are never satisfied with what they have. They pout, whine, and complain because they want a new toy or some more candy. If they happen to be making a big scene when we are in their vicinity, we might roll our eyes and wonder a little about the way their parents are raising them. (And deep down, we might even be pleased that it is someone else's kids or grandkids and not our own this time!)

One thing worse than seeing a spoiled child act up is interacting with a grown-up who takes everything they have for granted. Oh, they probably don't scream or hold their breath to get what they want, but it's still not pleasant. Nothing will diminish your life more quickly and profoundly than being ungrateful. I know rich people who are miserable in the midst of their many belongings.

Conversely, nothing will enlarge your life more quickly and dramatically than gratitude. I know poor people who are convinced they are rich, recognizing and savoring their many blessings.

Do you want to know the cure for anger, bitterness, resentment, jealousy, low self-esteem, a quarreling spirit, and other modern maladies? Do you want to live a better life? It's really simple. Be grateful for what you have.

In the 100th Psalm—a Bible passage we should all take to heart—King David leads the people of his nation in worship of God. Not only does he tell them to have a thankful attitude in their hearts, but he says that they must say it aloud and "give thanks." David knows the real reasons for gratitude:

- *We have been created by God and belong to Him (100:3).*
- *The Lord is good and His love endures forever (100:5).*

Does this mean that everything went right for David? Hardly. His life was filled with heartache and disappointment. There were times he lived in a state of depression and near despair. And yet, he understood that even in the "valley of the shadow of death" (Psalm 23:4), God was always near to comfort and bless him. David saw God's gracious hand in his life—and thanked Him.

How often do you slow down to think about how

blessed your life really is? Do you look at your world with eyes of wonder and appreciation? With thankfulness?

A thankful heart leads to a great life, because even in the midst of challenges in our work, our home, our relationships, and our personal development, the thankful heart realizes that God's world is full of blessings and miracles.

> *Oh, give thanks to the Lord, for He is good!*
> *For His mercy endures forever.*
>
> 1 CHRONICLES 16:34

Live with Purpose by ...

Keeping a Sense of Humor

*Those who bring sunshine into the lives
of others cannot keep it from themselves.*

JAMES MATTHEW BARRIE

For over twenty-five years, the late Johnny Carson entertained millions of Americans at bedtime. We never got tired of watching him, probably because his best material wasn't from a script, but was based on his spontaneous interaction with his guests. No matter what they had to say, he could always turn it into something very funny and entertaining. Obviously, few people are gifted with that kind of talent, but everyone can have a sense of humor.

I don't remember the best jokes I've heard, and even when I do, I don't tell them that well. The writer of Proverbs tells us: "A merry heart does good, like medicine" (17:22). So I laugh, I smile, I tell jokes poorly, tease, and enjoy the lighter side of life!

Yes, life is serious and we can't joke around all the time, but that doesn't mean we always have to be somber. In his classic little book, *Man's Search for Meaning*, Viktor E. Frankl, a renowned Viennese psychiatrist—and a Jewish survivor of the Auschwitz death camp—teaches us that one of the keys to mental health and experiencing life fully is laughter. I believe him.

In my Wal-Mart days, we worked hard, but we always had fun in our work—and I can tell you that work and fun are not mutually exclusive. Sam Walton was very effective at using humor and wasn't afraid to poke a little fun at himself. If sales were soft or we were going through a difficult time, Sam would lead a crazy sing-along or a talent show at our Saturday morning manger's meeting to liven everyone up. His hula dance on Wall Street—in response to our associates achieving a particularly high year-end goal—has been widely reported over the years.   Some smirked at what they thought was a simple publicity stunt, probably in large measure because they simply didn't know the kind of man Sam was.   His associates loved it, it built up morale, and he liked a good laugh. Humor was a part of my everyday life in Wal-Mart and I think it made us much more effective.

I hope humor is part of your life, too.   It takes a positive attitude and a strong desire to enjoy life to see the humor around us—but having a little laughter sprinkled throughout your day is a great way to live.   I might add, the only way to really live.

A merry heart does good, like medicine,

But a broken spirit dries the bones.

PSALM 17:22

Live with Purpose by ...

Being Optimistic

It is difficult to say what is impossible, for the dream of yesterday is the hope of today and the reality of tomorrow.

ROBERT H. GODDARD

Being optimistic means that you have a positive attitude in all that you do—and optimism will have a major impact on what you accomplish in life. Successful people are people who think positively and believe they can influence the outcome of the circumstances of life. Optimistic people say to themselves, "I can do it and, in fact, I will do it."

Every year at Wal-Mart, we had a different annual theme. A few years ago, our theme was "Imagine the Possible." In preparation for my presentation to all our store managers about the new theme, I thought

about the words "possible" and "impossible." I
realized that the word "impossible" restricted our
thinking about what we were capable of doing. Many
other companies could have achieved what Wal-Mart
had, but they didn't. Why? I believe they thought
what Wal-Mart had accomplished was really impossible, so they never tried. How sad!

I looked the word "impossible" up in the
dictionary and found the following definition: "Felt to
be incapable of being done, attained, or fulfilled."
The phrase in this definition that jumped off the page
at me was "felt to be." It didn't mean that it couldn't
be done, but rather that it hadn't been done and didn't
seem possible. It is a restriction that we place on
ourselves, thereby cutting off our full potential. As
Charles Chestnutt said, "Impossibilities are merely
things of which we have not learned, or which we do
not wish to happen."

There have been many events in history that were

perceived to be impossible but have been accomplished.

In the 1950s two Harvard scientists conclusively proved that space travel was impossible because of the weight of the fuel needed to create sufficient boost, only to be disproved a decade later when the United States landed men on the moon and got them back to Earth. The answer was really quite simple. Once the fuel had done its work, have that "stage" of the rocket with its weight and drag, break free.

Performing a heart transplant seemed like science fiction when I was growing up. *Impossible!* Dr. Christian Bernard of South Africa did it for the first time in 1967, and today organs are being transplanted thousands of times a day all across the world.

Think about the creation of Disneyland and Disney World. A major, national theme park concept was a new and risky undertaking. When Walt Disney unveiled his vision, there were plenty of nay sayers and critics. But he succeeded and created a completely new kind of entertainment experience that has changed the travel patterns of tourists from across the globe and helped build vacation paradises in Orlando, Florida, Anaheim, California, and even Europe and Asia, for the young and old alike.

When Fred Smith, founder of Federal Express, came up with the idea of sending a package from anywhere in the country to any other city overnight, not many believed it could be done. In fact, one of his business professors gave him a low mark for his business plan, which he first wrote as a class assignment. Now Federal Express is one of the most common means of shipping for individuals and businesses in our country and around the globe—and we can't imagine a world where we would have to actually wait a couple days to get a package we need now.

These achievements were all perceived to be impossible, but they were accomplished—and more and grander accomplishments were built on them. If these things were possible, what else is possible in your world that seems impossible to you today?

Norman Vincent Peale writes, "Become a possibilitarian. No matter how dark things seem to be or actually are, raise your sights and see possibilities—always see them, for they're always there."

Are there goals for you that you think are unattainable that in actuality could be achieved? If you have the faith to recognize what others believe to be impossible is actually possible, you can open up the boundaries of your mind, and who knows what you may be able to do?

If you have faith as a mustard seed, you will say to this mountain, "Move from here to there," and it will move; and nothing will be impossible for you.

MATTHEW 17:20

Live with Purpose by ...

Loving Others

Whatever outward service or obedience we render to
God or man, if love is withheld, the law is not fulfilled.

FREDERICK B. MEYER

If you graduated from an Ivy League college with highest honors and were awarded a full scholarship to study abroad for a year, but don't have love in your life, do your educational credentials really matter?

If you started your own business, which is skyrocketing in an upward growth trajectory, or took a job with a Fortune 500 company and have experienced a steady stream of promotions and raises, but don't have love in your life, do your impressive business accomplishments really matter?

If you invent the next generation of wireless

technology or create a revolutionary new system for inventory control and handling, but don't have love in your life, does your brilliance really matter?

We live in a society that lets its values get turned upside down and its priorities slide out of whack. We love money and use people. We crave more time and space for ourselves, but live in disconnected and lonely families. We chase after possessions until we no longer own them, but they own us.

When Jesus was asked by a religious leader of his day to distill the absolute, number one, most important commandment, he answered by saying: "'You shall love the Lord your God with all your heart, with all your soul, and with all your mind.' This is the first and great commandment. And the second is like it: 'You shall love your neighbor as yourself'" (Matthew 22:37-39). When Paul wrote his letter to the Corinthian church, apparently a group of new Christians who were quite proud of their sophisticated culture, their intelli-

gence, and their spiritual gifts, he said to them:
"Though I speak with the tongues of men and of
angels, but have not love, I have become sounding
brass or a clanging cymbal.   And though I have the gift
of prophecy, and understand all mysteries and all
knowledge, and though I have all faith, so that I could
remove mountains, but have not love, I am nothing.
And though I bestow all my goods to feed the poor,
and though I give my body to be burned, but have not
love, it profits me nothing" (1 Corinthians 13:1-3).

Does love of God and love for others permeate your
life?   I'm not talking about an emotional state of always
feeling happy and affectionate when you're close to
others, but an active lifestyle of interest, care, and
kindness toward others. To live greatly is to love greatly.

And now abide faith, hope, love,
these three; but the greatest of these is love.

1 CORINTHIANS 13:13

Live with Purpose by...

Doing Things Right

I've met a few people in my time who were enthusiastic about hard work. And it was just my luck that all of them happened to be men I was working for at the time.

BILL GOLD

I'm not really what you'd call a cowpoke, but I was inspired one day when I heard the famous Texas cowboy poet Red Steagall quote his poem, "The Fence that Me and Shorty Built." It's a poem about a would-be cowboy who is asked to help build a fence. He thinks fence-building is beneath him, after all he was hired to drive cattle and rope steers. And so as he begrudgingly starts digging post holes, he starts cutting corners. He goes around the rocks rather than digging them up and finds other ways to make the job easier.

As the rest of the crew starts setting posts, Shorty, a wise old cowboy and the foreman, notices that the fence zigs and zags haphazardly. It's definitely not straight, the way they marked it out. So he pulls our young cowpoke aside for a talk and says:

> *Now we could let it go like this*
> *And take the easy route.*
> *But doin' things the easy way*
> *Ain't what it's all about.*

> *If you're not proud of what you do,*
> *You won't amount to much.*
> *You'll bounce around from job to job*
> *Just slightly out of touch.*

Shorty convinces the cowboy to go back and fix his mistakes. He reminds him that not only will he save his job today, but on another day, years from now, he'll ride by and see a straight, durable fence and be able to point with pride to his work.

All of us have assignments, jobs, and responsibilities that we don't enjoy as much as others—and that don't bring us as much respect as others. Still, like the cowboy in the poem, we have a lot to learn from difficult, less rewarding jobs:

- *Do whatever you're asked to do—no job is so small or menial that it doesn't need to be done well. And no one is too good for the small jobs.*
- *Do things right the first time—it doesn't matter how hard you work if you're working on the wrong thing. Shortcuts usually end up costing time and quality—and reputation.*
- *Your attitude affects everyone around you—attitude is contagious, and a positive attitude can make the difference between a task completed with excellence and shoddy workmanship.*

- *Take pride in what you do—remember, your name is on every "fence" you build. In everything you do, do your best so that you can look back on your work with pride.*
- *Go back and correct your mistakes—we all make mistakes. The wise person admits them, corrects them, and doesn't leave them for others to take care of.*

What about you? Are you working with excellence in all areas of your work and life—or are you letting some tasks slide because you don't enjoy them as much as others? Can you look back on everything you've done in the past six months with pride?

Remember: "Doin' things the easy way ain't what it's all about."

> *Whatever your hand finds to do,*
> *do it with your might.*
>
> ECCLESIASTES 9:10

Live with Purpose by ...

Choosing to Be Joyful

The art of being happy lies in the power of
extracting happiness from common things.

HENRY WARD BEECHER

I was sitting at the kitchen table in my home, jotting down a few thoughts for a section of this book and half listening to the news that was airing on the television set in another room. The news reports that droned in the background included the usual mixture of catastrophes—another earthquake in the Philippines, a teenager who opened fire on fellow students at his high school, lawsuits and counter lawsuits within a family over ongoing life support measures, and more. Whew. Heavy stuff. I had to sigh. Life can be so hard and unfair. I was distracted from writing. But as

I started to rise and looked up, I saw a plaque that my wife had recently put up on the wall in front of me. On it were the simple words: Scatter Joy.

I sat back down. I asked myself, do I scatter joy? Do I even understand true joy? Of course, I understand and talk about *happiness* a lot, and my family and I certainly have much to be happy about. But happiness is based on circumstances, and I know too well on a personal level, I'm not as happy when things aren't going the way I want them to go. As I thought of the tragedies I had heard on the news, as I thought about the amount of time I think about my own happiness, I realized that there is something very different about joy than happiness.

Joy is not based on circumstances. You can experience a deep abiding joy no matter what you have to be happy or unhappy about in your world. Joyful people radiate something that is based in their heart and will. Others sense it and feel uplifted. I realized that's what "Scatter Joy" is all about. And I realized that I can't scatter joy unless I am joyful myself.

How much true joy do you see on a typical day in your life? I know it's not nice, but I almost have to laugh at some of the people I see. They look absolutely miserable. They shake their fists, yell, and blast their car horns in traffic. They mutter, scowl, and shift on their feet impatiently because someone in front of them at the convenience store is moving a little slow. I even see them at church, singing hymns about God's amazing grace, all the while looking like they just swallowed a lemon.

How about you? Do you want to live to make a difference? If so, you have to be different than those who go with the flow, and one key way to stand out is to be joyful! There are so many ways to experience God's joy in your life—no matter what is on the news and no matter how slow traffic is on your way to work. How many ways are you celebrating right now?

The joy of God's presence.   In Psalm 16:8-9 (NCV), David exalts: "I keep the Lord before me always. Because he is close by my side, I will not be hurt.   So I rejoice and am glad."   If God is beside you, no one can steal that joy.

The joy of salvation.   Paul tells us: "And not only that, but now we are also very happy in God through our Lord Jesus Christ.   Through him we are now God's friends again" (Romans 5:11 NCV). Forgiveness of sins and peace with God are great reasons to be joyful.

The joy of God's goodness.   Isaiah 63:9 tells us of God's great redemptive work: "In all their affliction He was afflicted, And the Angel of His Presence saved them; In His love and in His pity He redeemed them; And He bore them and carried them All the days of old."   What a kind and good God—and what a great source of joy!

The joy of God's Word.   King David speaks of God's

Word with awe, reverence, and joy: "I delight to do Your will, O my God, and Your law is within my heart" (Psalm 40:8). Do you set yourself up for joy each day by partaking of God's Word?

The joy of a clean heart. One of the most beautiful prayers ever uttered was David's immortal prayer for cleansing: "Create in me a pure heart, God, and make my spirit right again. Do not send me away from you or take your Holy Spirit away from me. Give me back the joy of your salvation. Keep me strong by giving me a willing spirit" (Psalm 51:10-12 NCV). If you are not experiencing joy in your life, maybe you need to start by seeking God's forgiveness and cleansing.

Joy in suffering. It doesn't seem possible to experience joy in the midst of sorrow, but Jesus reminded His disciples, "In the world you will have tribulation; but be of good cheer, I have overcome the world" (John 16:33).

Things do go wrong in our family life and our jobs from time to time. We're not supposed to be happy about everything that happens to us and in our world. But life's too short to succumb to a spirit of negativity. Sometimes it takes a decision, an act of the will to be joyful—and then God plants something real and abiding in our hearts.

Are you discouraged? Blue? Depressed? Don't forget—joy is everywhere!

> *Rejoice in the Lord always.*
>
> *Again I will say, rejoice!*
>
> PHILIPPIANS 4:4

Live with Purpose by ...

Keeping Humble

A great man is always willing to be little.

RALPH WALDO EMERSON

It was the August after I'd joined Wal-Mart, and I was about to get my first lesson in the ways of Sam Walton. We were opening three stores in Huntsville, Alabama. We had acquired two stores from another chain on opposite sides of the city. Not knowing we were going to acquire that company, we had already purchased land in the center of Huntsville for a Wal-Mart store there. Now we were on our way to participate in the grand opening of all three stores on the same day.

Sam went to the north store and I went to the south store. He cut the ribbon on the north and I cut the ribbon on the south. We met at the store in the

center of town.   We greeted customers, toured the
store, and shook hands with associates.   The store
looked great and we wanted to thank our associates for
doing such an excellent job.

Like most of the grand openings, we expected a big
crowd, but in this one our productivity couldn't keep up
with the traffic flow.   Before long, Sam jumped in and
began to bag merchandise.   He handed out candy to the
kids and did anything he could think of to help the
customers feel more comfortable with the long lines.

Sam got on the PA repeatedly, asking, "Anybody
need anything?"   He would then continue, "We are so
sorry that you are being held up today.   Next week
things will settle down and the lines won't be so long.
Thank you for coming to our grand opening today and
being patient with us."   He would then make a beeline
to someone who needed help.

I confess, as a former company president of a
national retail chain and now an executive vice presi-

dent for Wal-Mart, I had never served customers on the front lines like I did that day. You don't think I was going to stand around and watch my leader, do you?

Sam was a very humble man and he taught me a valuable lesson that day. None of us are too good to do the little jobs. In fact, there are no little jobs. If the Chairman of the Board wasn't too high and mighty to hand out lollipops and bag goods—neither was I.

There is much talk these days about being a servant leader, but I'm afraid that there's much more talk than action. We need to understand that our actions are the only thing that really counts. No matter how large we became, Sam always reminded us that we were no better than anyone else and should never become blinded by our own importance.

A potential danger of being a leader is that we can begin to think that we have all of the answers. After all, we have achieved an important position, we think, and we're above taking advice and doing those so-called "little" jobs. Unfortunately, I have seen too many leaders develop a large ego. Large egos frequently lead to arrogance, and when people become arrogant, their judgment can become impaired. Impaired judgment usually leads to failure.

We can see many examples of humility in the Scriptures—it is clear in Christ's teachings and in His life that we are to be humble people and put others first. When we do that, we honor God—but we also live a life of purpose and fulfillment.

By the way, in the process of having fun that day in Huntsville, I learned another life lesson I'll never forget: Humility is a marvelous partner to joy. I hope you will discover the joy of serving others.

> *Whoever desires to become great*
> *among you, let him be your servant.*
>
> MATTHEW 20:26

Live with Purpose by ...

Having a Personal Mission

Great minds have purposes, others have wishes.

WASHINGTON IRVING

When we started the Soderquist Center for Leadership and Ethics at John Brown University, it was because of concern about the deterioration in ethical standards in our country—the blurring of right and wrong.   The ethical issues we have in business today are not limited to a business problem, but reflect a problem with our whole society.   The Enron debacle may be what makes the front page of newspapers, but there is significant moral erosion in every corner of modern culture—education, politics, and sports.

Frequently when I meet with business groups, I ask them if they think that ethical practices today are the same as or worse then they were ten years ago. The vast majority of the leaders (usually over 90%) say that the landscape of today's business ethics is worse then ten years ago. Many suggest that we have lost our moral compass.

And so I have dedicated myself to raising yellow flags and even red flags with as many business leaders as possible. We are attempting to have a transforming impact on the way people in business and other organizations think and lead. We are challenging leaders to build their organizations on a sound foundation of values. The truth is, I find that the majority of people are concerned about what they see and hear. We're trying to encourage people to do something about it.

We are passionate about making a difference. We are reaching company leaders, not because of their status, but because of the incredible influence that they have on so many people in their organizations. If we can reach CEOs and senior leaders, then we can have an impact on the business. If we can have an impact on business, we have a much better chance of making an impact on individuals and their families. If we impact individuals and families, we can impact society at large.

Why am I telling you this? So you know what a good guy I am? Not hardly. I'm telling you this because I want you to know it's what gets me up every morning with a smile on my face—whether I've had my first cup of coffee or not—ready to go to work and battle. I'm supposed to be enjoying my retirement years—and I am! I love my work with business leaders so much that I'm not sure it's really work. I want my life to count for something, and you do too.

There's no better way to live your life than with a personal sense of mission!

I have obeyed the voice of the Lord, and gone on the mission on which the Lord sent me.

1 SAMUEL 15:20

Live with Purpose by...

Living Your Values

It's not hard to make decisions
when you know what your values are.

ROY DISNEY

What's the big deal about values? Are my personal
values really important? Many have pointed out that
there is much discussion over values in America today—
some would say we're practically at war over our values.
The debate is seen in entertainment, politics, religion—
every arena of life.

I frequently ask leaders if they know what their
personal values are—most say yes. Then I ask them:
"Have you ever written them down?" Most say no.

Values are incredibly important! They represent
what we believe and, in fact, determine who we really

are—what our character is, the real "you" when the mask is off. Therefore, values determine how we act. We act in accordance with what we believe.

I looked the word "values" up in numerous dictionaries, and they all were a little different. The definition I thought best describes what I'm trying to say went like this: "The beliefs that people have about what is right and wrong and what is most important in life, which control their behavior."

Where do our values come from? I know for myself that there have been many influences in my life that have impacted who I am and the values I hold. It began with my mom and dad, who were God-fearing people. They weren't any more perfect than you or I, but they did teach me what was right and wrong by what they said and how they lived. Their life lessons were simple and uncomplicated—it's wrong to lie, cheat, and steal, and you should follow the Golden Rule: Treat others the way you would like to be treated.

They also taught me that there was a God who loved me and that I should love Him and follow His directions as found in the Bible. They taught me that there were consequences if I did wrong.

The interesting thing was that my teachers in school, my friends, relatives, and neighbors, my Sunday school teachers, my pastor, and basically everyone I knew believed pretty much the same things. And when I went to study at Wheaton College, my values and beliefs were once again reinforced by what I heard and saw there. I realize that not everyone growing up when I did had the same reinforcement that I had, but many did.

Now, I don't want you to think that my upbringing was perfect—it wasn't. I was naïve about things like discrimination. I was unaware of what minorities had to live with, and that was wrong. I saw prejudice from a distance and didn't get involved. I see things more clearly today, and I am pleased to observe that we have made progress as a nation, but recognize that we still have a long way to go. Growing in my understanding and compassion in the area of prejudice has strengthened my values.

Other life experiences—seeing others suffer, seeing individuals mistreated in the workplace, seeing cold indifference and lack of compassion for those in need—have reinforced many of my early learnings about treating everyone with respect and dignity. I'm still learning and hope I never stop.

What I think is most important to understand is that the real key to values in our lives isn't so much what we say. The heart of our values is in what we do and how we do it. In other words, how are we living our lives? We can talk all we want, but the bottom line is what we do every day.

Always be ready to give a defense to everyone who asks you a reason for the hope that is in you.

1 PETER 3:15

PART TWO

LEARN AS A WAY OF LIFE

*And do not be conformed to this world, but
be transformed by the renewing of your
mind, that you may prove what is that good
and acceptable and perfect will of God.*

ROMANS 12:2

*A child-like man is not a man whose development has
been arrested; on the contrary, he is a man who has
given himself a chance of continuing to develop long
after most adults have muffled themselves in the
cocoon of middle-aged habit and convention.*

ALDOUS HUXLEY

Learn as a Way of Life from ...

Feeling a Sense of Wonder

He who can no longer pause to wonder and stand
rapt in awe, is as good as dead; his eyes are closed.

ALBERT EINSTEIN

It is wonderful to have grandchildren because they help us regain a sense of wonder when we see their eyes light up over very little things. To the very young, the beautiful wrapping paper on Christmas presents is almost as much fun as the presents themselves. It is delightful to watch their rapt attention as they follow a line of tiny ants trooping across the sidewalk and down a little dirt hole. I have cherished moments of seeing my grandkids perched on their tippy-toes to catch snowflakes on their tongues, squinting as snow falls in their eyes. Even our family dog, Charlie, an unusually intelligent black lab, dramatically experiences their wonder as they just screech in sheer delight every time they come visit me and Grandma and first walk in our house.

As we get older we begin to lose that wonder and awe over not only the little things, but also significant wonders of our world: the changing of the seasons, the beautiful sunrise and sunset, the fresh fallen snow on evergreen branches, the chirping of birds in the morning, the mist rising up from the meadows on cold frosty morning, the farmers' fields that are tilled or planted in neat rows and the little children I saw in Tokyo, Japan during cherry blossom time who stopped on the sidewalk to pick up the fallen blossoms and throw them high in the air to see them flicker back down to the ground. I think that Michael Yaconelli painted a beautiful word picture about awe—one that many of us can easily imagine from our own childhood experiences—in his book, *Dangerous Wonder*:

When I was six years old, my favorite comic book character was Superman. I admired his strength, his X-ray vision, his colorful uniform and bright red cape. What captured my imagination most was Superman's ability to fly. Many of my childhood fantasies were about flying. I honestly believed flying was still a possibility. I would talk my friends into playing Superman, and they would play for a while, but soon they would tire of the game because I wouldn't let anyone else be Superman. I had to be Superman, I told them, because I knew more about flying than they did.

Sneaking into my parent's bathroom, I would find the stash of forbidden towels (the thick, new ones reserved only for guests). Once outside, with the towel tied around my neck and dragging on the dirt behind me, I would run as fast as I could and jump off the highest survivable launching pad I could find. With arms outstretched, cape billowing behind me, wind rushing past my ears, I believed I was flying.

Then came a day when, without warning, without provo-

cation, I woke up, never to wear a "cape" again. Wherever the knowledge came from, it came nonetheless, and from that moment on I knew flying was nothing more than a childhood fantasy. I would never fly…and there is no Superman.

In retrospect, my day of "enlightenment" was a very sad day. I know now that something inside of me died that day. Whatever the "something" was, it was the stuff of dreams and imagination—the place where dancing, singing, laughter, and playing lived. Even at six, I understood that the possibility of flying wasn't the point: it was the alive-ness I felt when I thought I could fly; it was the voice I heard deep inside—a warm and loving voice, a living, believing voice, I recognized who it was: God. But that day, when I was just six years young my God-hearing went bad.

When was the last time you admired the setting sun or rising moon? When was the last time you strolled through a gallery to admire artwork? When was the last time you watched a line of ants march down a dirt hole?   When was the last time you had a "wow" experience and shared it with someone else?

It is so easy to get wrapped up in the immediate concerns of life that we fail to see, hear, and experience the wonderful things around us.   As you work hard on your journey to success, don't leave behind your ability to appreciate life's simple pleasures.

Many, O Lord my God, are Your

wonderful works which You have done;

And Your thoughts toward us

cannot be recounted to You in order;

If I would declare and speak of them,

They are more than can be numbered.

PSALM 40:5

Learn as a Way of Life from ...

Imitating the Success of Others

You don't have to be a "person of influence" to be
influential.   In fact, the most influential people in my life
are probably not even aware of the things they've taught me.

SCOTT ADAMS

There is so much to be learned by watching how
other people conduct their lives.   In the business
world as well as in my personal life, I have encountered
so many people who have inspired me to do things
better and to actually become a better person.   Of
course, I also see people who do things that are hurtful
to others, who treat others as dispensable.   I guess you
could argue that they are teachers, too.   They certainly
teach me how not to act and be.

Simply watching people isn't enough, though.   We

don't grow as individuals just by observing others, but only by incorporating these life lessons into our own lives—both the good things and the things we should avoid. In this way, we become better people and impact others in a positive way. I like what one educator said: *Only doing is learning.*

Do you want to grow from a lifestyle of lifelong learning and be a positive influence on others? You can be if you learn from others. I can barely express adequate gratitude to mentors and colleagues like Sam Walton and too many others to name. Frankly, the ones I've named are modest and wouldn't want attention drawn to themselves. But my interactions with them taught me many lessons on honesty, fair but tough negotiating, grace under pressure, and more.

But one critical reality I'd like to stress here is that we can learn important life lessons from people of every walk of life—not just the generals and inventors and business moguls.

I received a note in the mail a number of years ago while still working at Wal-Mart that underscored this truth.

The first time someone asked, "Remember the lady who was always so friendly at the door of Wal-Mart?" her face jumped immediately to my mind. It soon became apparent that this was not an isolated experience—more than a few people knew this woman as the friendly face at the door of Wal-Mart.

In those first days after her death, no one seemed to know what her name was. But she had touched people and they remembered her. What a wonderful tribute to a lady who smiled, said hello, and asked if we needed a cart.

The lesson for us is that our actions, no matter how small, whether positive or negative, private or public, will impact others, perhaps far more than we ever imagine. This lady realized the power of that connectedness and utilized it. With smiles, words, and small gestures she was, in a few moments of contact, able to touch people.

If only we all could be remembered with such fondness by strangers who did not even know our name.

Wow! Talk about a powerful testimony. I can tell you that that unnamed woman not only touched the lives of hundreds who met her at the front door of that Wal-Mart store, but she touched my life as well. From the day that Doris Sutterer jotted these lines to me, I have made a conscious effort to smile, say hello, and be helpful. We can truly learn from others.

> *Brothers and sisters, all of you should try to follow my example and to copy those who live the way we showed you.*
>
> PHILIPPIANS 3:17 NCV

Learn as a Way of Life from ...

Evaluating Yourself Honestly

One must not hold one's self so divine as to be unwilling
occasionally to make improvements in one's creations.

LUDWIG VAN BEETHOVEN

I saw a couple of teenage girls at a store not too long ago. Their heads were bent close as they giggled and whispered together. Amused and curious, I looked in the direction that one of the girls pointed and sure enough, there were some nice looking boys their age.

It is a natural part of the human mind to evaluate almost everything we see everyday. We all evaluate musicians, athletes, our pastors, our bosses, and the people we work with. (And yes, teenage girls evaluate the appearance of teenage boys and vice-versa.)

An official evaluation process, either formal or

informal, takes place in most every company and organization in the country.   Whether we ever stop to think about it or not, everybody that we know or even come in contact with evaluates us on the basis of what they hear us say and see us do.

But do we ever take the time to seriously evaluate ourselves? That's hard to do—we're really not very objective about ourselves. And yet self-evaluation can be incredibly valuable in growing as a person and as a leader.

If we have a genuine desire to be the best that we can be, the self-evaluation process begins by honestly taking a time-intensive look at ourselves and determining what we are doing well and what we could do better. This cannot be done in fifteen minutes squeezed into a busy schedule in your office. You have to get away from phones and everyone else, preferably in some restful place where you can do some serious, uninterrupted thinking. If you are married and bold enough, ask your husband or wife to share their thoughts with you as a part of your preparation for a self-evaluation retreat. (Obviously, don't ask them right after or during an argument!)

But just evaluating yourself isn't enough. Once you've reached some conclusions about your effectiveness and execution, you have to decide what you need to do to improve—and what you are willing to do.

We all have strengths—but no one is perfect. Every one of us can improve and be more effective if we really want to. But we must be willing to honestly evaluate ourselves and then be determined to change. That's not easy—change is hard. In fact, change is very hard.

In Wal-Mart, we were constantly evaluating everything we did and looking for ways to improve, and didn't shy away from making major changes if that's what was needed. We called this process "Correction of Errors." Even after very successful holiday seasons, we would spend only a few minutes celebrating the good things that we did, but spent the majority of our time determining what we could do better.

Periodic self-evaluation is very healthy for every one of us, just like going to the doctor for an annual physical. You can catch things that are going wrong before they become more serious and take appropriate corrective action.

It's not easy to evaluate ourselves—and it's even harder to determine to make changes—but it's a commitment and process that can't be ignored if you want to do your best.

The good news is that the willingness to evaluate yourself means you have the humility and honesty to reach the next level in your life. The even better news is that you don't have to do it all on your own. God is always ready to hear our prayers and help us in our areas of need.

God began doing a good work in you, and I am sure he will continue it until it is finished when Jesus Christ comes again.

PHILIPPIANS 1:6 NCV

Learn as a Way of Life from ...

Listening

Courage is what it takes to stand up and speak;

courage is also what it takes to sit down and listen.

WINSTON CHURCHILL

Peter MacMahon, a Wal-Mart executive in Europe, told me about the following incident that happened when he was a young manager for a major retail conglomerate in England.

I was working for Lewis's, one of biggest departmental store groups in the UK. The shopping habits of the British consumer had changed in the previous decade, and our stores suffered sales and profit declines consistently for ten years.

I was in charge of the food division in the Manchester store in 1980, and was under constant pressure to reduce costs. I had decided to terminate a particular elevator operator in the goods receiving area.

David Flowers, who had operated the same goods elevator for thirty years, was, due to decreasing volumes, no longer required, and the plan was to let him go and close down the elevator he operated. On a Friday morning, the HR manager and I interviewed David and informed him his employment would be terminated and he would be compensated in line with company policy. He was devastated. I just considered it to be a necessary part of the job.

He left that Friday evening and took his personal belongings with him. On the following Monday, David came to work and was seen by members of the staff at his normal start time and duly proceeded to operate his lift. I was on leave that day so had no part in how the HR manager dealt with the situation. The manager told me that David was asked to leave, but argued that he had to do his job. He was eventually escorted out by security.

Over the course of the next few days David was seen by members of staff hanging around the streets outside the store all day, but nobody investigated why.

John Ridge, who was the HR director for all Lewis's stores and who had once been the HR manager of the Manchester store, heard of this situation from one of the HR assistants and came by train from London.   John was a great character.   In his lifetime, he had been a Major in the British Army and lead a regiment of the Gerkes in Nepal. He was a brave man who commanded a lot of admiration from the staff and respect from his superiors because of the values he held.   He came to the Manchester store and asked me to describe the details of what had happened and what we at the store had done to help David.   He listened intently to my version of events.   His questions were not focused on why we had let David go, but on what we had done to help him with this current crisis.

I had to admit I had not done a lot.

John then asked where David was and was told he

usually could be found somewhere outside the store. He left the store to find David and eventually returned with him and asked me to join them in the HR office. John asked David several questions and found out that the reason he had been coming to the store every day was that he could not bear to tell his wife he had lost his job because he was frightened of the affect it would have on her. He explained he had always done this job and his family was dependent on the income and stability of it. He described that he knew nothing else and was immensely frightened about the future and the impact the job loss would have on him personally. "What will I do all day?" he asked.

John was honest, he told David the reasons why the job had to go, and that he could not change that, but he persuaded David to agree on an action plan to try and find alternative solutions. John went home with David to explain to his wife what had happened and why. He charged the HR personnel to help David find another job and soon thereafter David found a position in another store in the area.   He asked me to arrange dinner with David and his friends and family as a farewell gesture from the company.

This incident was personally mortifying and embarrassing for me, but had a great bearing on my own values and the way I have tried to act as a manager since then.   John taught me the value of being open and honest, treating others with dignity, being supportive, getting personally involved in specific situations, and the simple power of listening.

Watching him asking questions of David in that office—and hearing him out—and the positive affect it had on the crisis, has helped me to never act boldly or rashly without listening again.

> So then, my beloved brethren, let every man be
> swift to hear, slow to speak, slow to wrath.
>
> JAMES 1:19

Learn as a Way of Life from ...

Praying

Prayer may not change things for you,
but it for sure changes you for things.

SAMUEL M. SHOEMAKER

Walking through a crowded airport, I saw a man kneeling reverently on a beautiful prayer rug, his head touching the ground, his body pointing toward the east. I was visibly reminded that all of the great faith traditions of the world affirm our need to pray. I was visibly reminded of my need to pray!

As a Christian, I draw great comfort and hope from Jesus' words that though He is physically removed from us, the Heavenly Father has left the Holy Spirit to live within us and energize our spiritual life—especially our prayer life (John 14:15-17). Jesus goes on to say that the Spirit is our "teacher" (John 14:26-27). Do you ever think of God as your Divine teacher? Think of the greatest teacher you have ever heard in your life—and then think of how much more God has to teach you.

I do believe that you will enrich not only your spiritual life, but also your mental—and even your physical—life through an active prayer life. Yes, when we pray, God acts on our behalf in the world, but I think it is more often the case that the greatest change is within us.

If prayer truly is conversation with a real, living, personal, listening, speaking God—and I believe it is— then the biggest need for most of us is learning to listen more. That can be a struggle for me. I know how to tell God I love Him and what I need help with. I'm not as good at being silent and waiting to hear what He has to say to me. I suspect I'm not alone.

Some things that might help you and me include:

- *Fill your mind with God's thoughts by reading your Bible as part of your prayer time.*
- *Reaffirm your belief that God does speak to us today.*
- *Take time to be silent—something that's oh so tough in our noise- and media-saturated society—as part of your prayer time.*
- *Keep your eyes and heart open throughout the day so you don't miss the unique and creative ways God wants to speak to you.*

If you want to grow through a lifestyle of learning, I can't think of a better source of wisdom than the God who is all-wise and all-knowing.

Rejoice always, pray without ceasing, in everything give thanks; for this is the will of God in Christ Jesus for you.

1 THESSALONIANS 5:16-18

Learn as a Way of Life from ...

Unlearning

*The illiterate of the 21st century will not be
those who cannot read and write, but those
who cannot learn, unlearn, and relearn.*

ALVIN TOFFLER

The old adage teaches us that practice makes
perfect.   But what if we practice doing things the
wrong way?   You can go through three or four buckets
of tennis balls every day to improve your serve, but
what if you were taught wrong technique from your
first instructor?

The two problems with what we learned yesterday
are that we might have gotten it wrong the first time—
and things change so that the old ways are no longer
necessarily the right ways.

When we introduced computer technology at Wal-Mart, our biggest challenge was not finding the hardware or programming the software to dramatically improve our operations. Our challenge was introducing new technology to people at every level of the company who were already very comfortable with how we were doing things at the present. We quickly discovered that in order to introduce major change, we not only needed to budget learning time, but also unlearning time.

I'm not one of those people who aren't happy unless there's major change in the air. I believe that when management constantly creates a state of flux and change, it is destabilizing and hurts morale. All of us, however, need to be ready to embrace positive changes—and that often requires the difficult and painful task of cutting off previous ways of thinking and doing.

God doesn't change. Well thought-through beliefs

and values don't change either.   But just about everything else in life is up for grabs—work processes and
systems, fashion, ways of communicating, and other
"derivative" activities.

For you to go to the next level in your thinking,
what do you need to let go of and unlearn?

> *Behold, I will do a new thing,*
>
> *Now it shall spring forth;*
>
> *Shall you not know it?*
>
> *I will even make a road in the*
>
> *wilderness and rivers in the desert.*

ISAIAH 43:19

Learn as a Way of Life from ...

Hearing Great Speakers

The wisdom of the wise and the experience

of the ages are perpetuated by quotations.

BENJAMIN DISRAELI

From time to time, we would invite an outside speaker to our Saturday meetings at Wal-Mart to share their leadership principles with us. Their comments tended to reinforce the Wal-Mart principles and had a powerful effect coming from outside our company by well-respected leaders. We invited some very well-known public figures like Warren Buffet, Tommy Franks, and others.

Celebrities and sports figures were sometimes invited by our suppliers to come and speak to the group, like Mary Lou Retton, Hank Aaron, Nolan Ryan,

Joe Montana, and Dan Marino. Musicians like Marie Osmond, Amy Grant, and Steven Curtis Chapman came and entertained the associates, but often shared their personal life principles with us as well. It was always exciting to have such prominent figures come and speak to us, but it was also a learning experience for all of us. Can you imagine getting all of these people to come to Bentonville, Arkansas, at 7:30 on a Saturday morning for any other reason than to speak to Wal-Mart leaders?

You don't have to be a manager at Wal-Mart to hear great speakers. There are countless opportunities all around you to hear exciting speakers, in both big and small settings. When was the last time you attended one of the following?

- Continuing education classes
- Leadership seminars
- Civic organizations
- Chamber of Commerce meetings

- Success seminars

- Special speakers in local churches

- Lectures open to the public at universities

Church attendance is down in America. Attend a typical trade seminar, and you might see more people milling around in the hallways than in the auditorium and break-out session rooms.

How about you? Are you actively looking for opportunities to hear great people share great messages? Is it too much trouble? Do you pop a motivational tape in your car stereo system on a long drive? Or is it easier to daydream and listen to music the whole time? Are you taking advantage of all the great presentations and opportunities to learn around you?

Listen to counsel and receive instruction,
That you may be wise in your latter days.

PROVERBS 19:20

Learn as a Way of Life from ...

Finding Great Role Models

*The most important single influence in the life of a
person is another person who is worthy of emulation.*

PAUL D. SHAFER

All of us are different. We are unique in our looks
and personalities, our thoughts, and how we view life.
But one area where I think we are all similar is that
most of us look up to and respect certain people in our
lives. For some, it may be a mom or dad or uncle. For
others, it may be a teacher, a youth leader, or pastor. For
even others, it may be a celebrity—a sports hero, an
actor, or a singer. We like them because of their talent,
the way they look, the way they do what they do, the
way they dress, or even the way they make us feel. We
like them so much we may dress or act or talk like them.

They become our role models.

Do you have any role models? As you were growing up or even now today, have there been people you admire and want to be like? I think it is healthy to have role models—they can provide a standard for us to look up to and can be an inspiration to us to be better and achieve more than we would on our own.

Because a role model can be an enormous influence on how we think and act, it is critical to select the correct individual to model ourselves after. It is very possible, and we see examples of it almost every day, to pick someone who may influence us negatively and influence us to do wrong things.

Besides my mom and dad, Sam Walton has had the greatest influence on my life. He was very bright, passionate, and full of energy. He enjoyed life. He treated everyone with respect and dignity. He was a lifetime learner. He always wanted to know other people's opinions and was an excellent listener.

I heard the follow story shared by the pastor of a little church in Colorado:

Dave Crane's parents served as missionaries in Hoi Ping, China, where Dave was born and lived until he was nine years old. Before returning to the States, Dave's father and a Chinese pastor built a church in a small, rural village called Long Bui.

Dave followed in his father's footsteps as a missionary, serving faithfully in Trinidad for thirty-five years. As he and his wife were reaching retirement, their mission organization asked them to return to Hong Kong for a short-term assignment to fill a vacancy. While Dave was in China, he thought it would be great to visit his home village and try to find the church his father had built.

As he was walking around the village where they had built the church, he noticed an old man and woman walking straight towards him. When the old man got up to him, he said, "K dok san?"—his father's Chinese name. Dave replied, "No, K Dai Wai," which was his own Chinese name.

Over the years, Dave had come to look like his father and

*walk like his father and talk like his father, whom the old man
remembered and admired.*

We joke that dog owners and their dogs begin to look
alike over time. We laugh when we say, "I'm becoming
just like my parents." But I like that story of a missionary
kid who became a great missionary himself because it
reminded me how much we can improve ourselves by
following in the footsteps of excellent role models.

The ultimate role model for us to follow is Jesus
Christ. The term "Christian" literally means "Christ like."
As we grow and mature spiritually, our very image, how
we think and act, should be changing to look more and
more like His.

Who are you looking up to today?

Imitate me, just as I also imitate Christ.

1 CORINTHIANS 11:1

Learn as a Way of Life from ...

Reading Great Books

You are the same today that you are going to be five years from now except for two things: the people with whom you associate and the books you read.

CHARLES "TREMENDOUS" JONES

The average American reads less than one book a year. It makes me wonder who in the world is buying and digesting those 25,000 new titles that release each year in our country alone!

Could it be that when it comes to acquiring new knowledge the rich are getting richer? (And the poor are getting poorer?)

There are so many benefits to reading. Of course, the fact that you are holding a book in your hands right now means that you already know that. But consider just four of the ways that a consistent reading plan will enhance your life:

- Mental exercise—when you watch television, you don't have to engage your imagination or the full range of thought processes required with reading. Maybe that's why so many choose not to read; it's a little harder. But just as physical exercise makes you stronger, reading makes you mentally sharper.
- Deeper levels of thinking—we gather so much of our understanding of the world through TV and radio, yet the material tends to be presented in quick, attention-grabbing sound bites.   Books and other forms of print media can go much deeper into a topic. As you read about important subjects, you can challenge your own thinking—and grow intellectually.
- More interesting conversation—no one likes an intellectual snob or showoff, but face it: When you read you become a more interesting conversationalist.

• Spiritual development—when Gutenberg invented the printing press to produce the Bible for the common man, he forever linked the printed word with spiritual growth.

There are so many great books to choose from in every category of interest you have—political science, Christian living, history, mystery and adventure, humor, and technical subjects! Pick areas that are positive. When you read a novel, can you find principles for living? What do we learn from the past? Read what you like—and push yourself to grow by trying new areas.

I would note that I've always believed reading is an excellent way to learn about leadership—I always encouraged our management team at Wal-Mart to develop their own library of good business and personal development books. Let me challenge you to set your own goals and stick to them. I also challenge you to return to your college days and underline or highlight the points that make the biggest impression on you and to refer back to those highlighted areas often. What's reasonable for you? A book each month? One a week? Four or five a year?

Finally, don't forget God's Word. David, one of the grandest leaders of all time, said "When I remember You on my bed, I meditate on You in the night watches" (Psalm 63:6). What a great way to start and end your day! And Peter tells us to "always be ready to give a defense to everyone who asks you a reason for the hope that is in you" (1 Peter 3:15).

I recently bought a new computer. In order to set it up correctly, I had to carefully consult the instruction packet that came with the computer. After I got it set up, I didn't know how to use it until I read more of the instruction book. I still have to look up how to use certain functions.

I couldn't live my spiritual life without the ultimate

instruction manual for life—the Bible. The Bible showed me how to get started, showed me where my source of power was and how to get connected with that power.

There are many stories in the Bible that have modeled for me the things I should and should not do—in short, how I should live my life. I could never have operated my computer without reading the instruction manual, and I could never live the spiritual life without consistently reading the Bible.

Nurture your mind and soul with great books.

The judgments of the Lord are true; they are completely right. They are worth more than gold, even the purest gold. They are sweeter than honey, even the finest honey.

PSALM 19:9-10 NCV

Learn as a Way of Life from …

Being Willing to Change

Not all organizations adapt equally well to the environment within which they grow. Many, like the dinosaur of great size but little brain, remain unchanged in a changing world.

CHARLES HANDY

Change is hard. Let me put that differently. Change is very hard.

Change may be one of the hardest things we do, but it is essential that we have an open mind and heart to change, or we will stagnate and miss out on becoming all that we can become. That doesn't mean that we should change just for the sake of change, which drives everyone around us crazy and really doesn't accomplish anything but a lack of commitment to new programs since everyone knows they are going to whimsically change again anyway.

There needs to be a purpose behind every change we make. But we do need to curb our natural tendency to do things the way we always have. It is in our willingness to change that we discover new and better ways to live, learn, and lead.

I was at a banquet one evening and had the opportunity to visit with Harry Cunningham, the former CEO of K-Mart stores. In fact, he was the legendary character who dramatically changed retail in America by developing the concept of the K-Mart stores for the former Kresge company—a model that we carefully studied and considered when developing Wal-Mart stores. I thanked him for what he had done in pioneering the successful discounting format as we know it today. He was very gracious in accepting my praise, but was quick to add how much he appreciated what Wal-Mart had done in developing the concept even further.

He went on to say, "We made a serious mistake along the way by not changing and updating our stores over the years. We had a successful formula that was working and saw no reason to change. You folks at Wal-Mart continued to improve until you were much better than we were, and by that time, you passed us by."

The lesson for me in that conversation was that while success can lead to success, it could also lead to failure if you refuse to focus on improving.

In Wal-Mart, we had what we called a low "RC factor"—that is a low Resistance to Change. Over time we continued to change—and hopefully improve—just about everything we did and how we did it. Sam built a team that was obsessed with better meeting the needs of customers through better stores, better prices, and better service.

One thing that we refused to change was our values. The core beliefs we had about treating people fairly, telling the truth, being honest in our dealings with everyone, keeping promises, being fair, and striving for excellence formed the foundation of how we interacted with each other as well as with people outside the company, including our customers.

Are you ready to lead your team to new heights? Then buckle your seatbelt because change is in the air.

He who keeps instruction is in the way of life,

But he who refuses correction goes astray.

PROVERBS 10:17

Learn as a Way of Life from ...

Being Passionate

A platoon leader doesn't get his platoon to go by getting up and shouting and saying, "I am smarter. I am bigger. I am stronger. I am the leader." He gets men to go along with him because they want to do it for him and they believe in him.

DWIGHT D. EISENHOWER

There have been a lot of books written about leadership—good books with many suggestions that are very valid. But I appreciate the simplicity of what Daniel Goleman says: "Great leaders *move us*. They *ignite our passion* and *inspire the best in us*."

That's what leaders do. They move us to do something that we wouldn't think to do on our own. They light the spark that causes us to get excited and really want to do what we're doing, to pour our whole selves into it. And they are the encourager who makes us strive for excellence and become all that we can become.

Leaders are the motivating force behind every major accomplishment—good and bad—the world has ever known. Churchill rallied the English people in the "darkest hour" of World War II to never surrender through his nightly radio broadcasts. Hitler incited the masses to destroy the shops of "undesirables" and burn books through his public oratory. Both men painted pictures in the minds of their followers of something powerful they could be a part of. But we're not talking about psychological manipulation and management technique. Because passion to be contagious must begin in your heart.

We have all sat under leaders who are very intelligent and can clearly see things that we don't, but have no ability—or desire—to transfer that picture into our minds. It's probably not because they can't communicate their vision. Oftentimes, the problem is that the vision they are attempting to articulate doesn't come from their heart, and we easily sense that. As a result, we aren't moved to make the vision a reality.

When we lead others, whether at work, in church, in educational settings, or in our families, our objective needs to be to get their commitment to the work at hand. People who are only complying with your requests or rules and regulations will, at best, do only what you ask them to do. People who are committed to your vision, on the other hand, will not only do what you ask, but go far beyond that and do all they possibly can to accomplish the goal.

We had a store manager who had a special passion for helping people grow. In his store in Manhattan, Kansas, a university town in which a lot of our associates were college students, he trained more young people for assistant and store manager positions than I believe anyone else in all of Wal-Mart. His leadership style just fostered a desire in young people to move forward and excel, and he was instrumental in helping students take off in significant Wal-Mart careers and with other companies. It wasn't his position, but his passion, that enabled him to have a greater impact on the development of young leaders than anyone else in Wal-Mart.

Do people follow you because of your position or title, or do they follow you because they believe in you, are committed to your lead, and want to follow? Do you move people, ignite their passion, and inspire them to be the best that they can be?

> *And whatever you do, do it heartily,*
> *as to the Lord and not to men.*
>
> COLOSSIANS 3:23

PART THREE

LEAD TO MAKE A DIFFERENCE

I will send you to Pharaoh that you may bring My people, the children of Israel, out of Egypt.

EXODUS 3:10

Leadership is about taking an organization to a place it would not have otherwise gone without you, in a value-adding, measurable way.

GEORGE M.C. FISHER

Every great institution is the lengthened shadow of a single man. His character determines the character of his organization.

RALPH WALDO EMERSON

Lead to Make a Difference by...

Creating Teamwork

The most important measure of how good a game I played

was how much better I'd made my teammates play.

BILL RUSSELL

If you can't tell by now, I love sports! I love the excitement of competition; the feeling of accomplishment when I have given my very best—win or lose.   Of course, giving my very best now is usually cheering enthusiastically for the basketball team my son coaches at John Brown University or when my grandchildren play soccer, basketball, or other sports!

There are great lessons to apply to life and leadership from sports. One of the most important ones is the power of teamwork. It isn't necessarily the team with the most superstars or highest payroll that wins the Super Bowl or World Series. A great team will often beat a group of highly talented individuals—even if they are loaded with superstars—because the true team has learned to play together.

Michael Jordan is my favorite professional basketball player. Some believe that he was the best to ever play the game. He clearly had a lot of God-given talent, but he multiplied his natural gifts by always working hard to improve.

As a young professional, Michael Jordan led the National Basketball Association in scoring six of his first seven years, averaging over thirty-seven points per game one season. That particular year his team had a losing season. The Bulls never won a championship during that first seven-year span. But the Bulls' ownership group kept adding key players to the team. Notice I said "key players" and not superstars. Some would even call those great Bulls teams of the nineties a rag-tag collection of players and personalities. But each player knew what he was good at and what he had to offer the team.   Winning became more important than individual awards and accolades.   Michael Jordan never again averaged as many points as he did early in his career.   But the Chicago Bulls won six NBA championships—the true measure of greatness.

Is the power of teamwork true just of sports? Absolutely not! I've seen it work over and over again in all walks of life. Sam Walton was a wonderful leader, but we had an incredible company. Wal-Mart is a wonderful example of ordinary people working together as a team and achieving extraordinary results. Oh, there were plenty of talented individuals, but what was most remarkable was the teamwork.

The Bible says that we are all one body made up of many parts. We need all the parts in order for the body to function properly. We can't all be arms or eyes or feet. We are made differently and therefore we complement each other. No one person has all the answers or can do it all. We accomplish much more if we know our own abilities, recognize that other people do some things better than we do, and understand that if we do our part and encourage others to do theirs, we will be successful.

Are you a team player? Could you accomplish more if you worked more closely with others? And why shouldn't we work alongside others, getting and giving help as needed? Teamwork is the quickest route to maximizing a group's potential.

We are many, but in Christ we are all one body.
Each one is a part of that body, and each
part belongs to all the other parts.

ROMANS 12:5 NCV

Lead to Make a Difference by...

Treating Everyone with Respect

Life is made up, not of great sacrifice or duties,
but of little things, in which smiles and kindness
and small obligations win and preserve the heart.

HUMPHREY DAVY

I was traveling in stores one day and stopped in a smaller store that had been open thirteen or fourteen years. While the store looked old and was very crowded, it was obvious that it was well operated and the associates were doing a good job of keeping the store neat and clean and well stocked.

After walking through and looking to see if I could offer any assistance, I met with a group of associates in the lunch room. I told them I thought they were doing a great job of keeping the store attractive and taking care of our customers. They were highly complimentary of how their manager treated them and without any prompting went on to add how much he cared about them as individuals. Many of the associates said that he was the best manager they ever had.

I asked them how they knew he cared for them. One of the ladies shared a simple story with the group. She said that several years before, when there was a different manager, her daughter was selected for the National Honor Society. The school was holding a special recognition ceremony the next evening for the students and their parents, and she was scheduled to work. When she went to her manager and explained the situation, it was obvious that he was unhappy. He gave her a rough time about it and said that she would have to find someone to take her place for the evening. He further told her to never let it happen again. She found another associate to work for her and did go to the school program, but on a night that should have been filled with joy over her daughter's accomplishment, she felt guilty and worried the whole time—like she had done something wrong.

She went on to say that she recently had a similar situation when her young son was selected to play in a Little League All-Star game on a day when she was scheduled to work. She went to the current manager and explained the situation. He told her that he thought that was wonderful and that she must be proud of her son. She quickly offered to find someone to take her place and he said she didn't have to do that, that he would take care of it himself. She went to the game and thoroughly enjoyed the evening. The following day, the manager made a beeline to her and asked how the game went and how her son had done.

In both cases, she went to her children's activities, but in one case she felt horrible, while in the other case she felt great. It was all in how her manager had responded to her request.

This lady's example impressed on me again how we can impact other people's feelings both for the good and for the bad through the way we express respect to them and by the way we treat them.

Everyone I know wants to be treated fairly, to feel that people respect them and genuinely care about them. It's easy to say that we respect other people, but sometimes our actions don't back up our talk. People in leadership positions should always show respect for everyone—but especially the people who work for them. When you demonstrate to people that you care about them, they will be much more inclined to follow you.

The adage is true: people don't care what you think until they know that you care.

> *When you do things, do not let selfishness or pride be your guide. Instead, be humble and give more honor to others than to yourselves.*
>
> **PHILIPPIANS 2:3 NCV**

Lead to Make a Difference by ...

Putting Values First

Good values are easier caught than taught.

ZIG ZIGLAR

When I first joined Wal-Mart, wherever I spoke, people wanted to know how Wal-Mart had managed to be so successful, though we were still quite a small company compared to the giant retailers of that day.   I usually shared off a list including our real estate strategy, our everyday low pricing, our merchandise assortment, our people programs—and numerous other business strategies.

After a while, I began to realize that these strategies weren't the ultimate root of our success.   For one thing, we certainly weren't the only company with good business practices.   And I came to realize that strategies, to be effective, had to be constantly fine-tuned.   But there was something much more fundamental that didn't change: the foundational beliefs and values of the company. It became apparent to me that everything we did grew out of our beliefs, and our beliefs grew out of our values.

In what is probably too cynical—but also, too often true—of a statement, J. Ian Morrison says, "Most organizations have values written by the marketing department, spoken by the CEO, and espoused by no one else in the organization." But because of Sam's relentless passion to instill certain values into his company—and I promise you, he talked and practiced his values from morning to night every single day—if you stop any associate in Wal-Mart and ask them what our three basic beliefs are, you will hear the following in their own words:

- *We treat everyone with respect and dignity.*
- *We are in business to satisfy our customers.*
- *We strive for excellence in all that we do.*

Now when I speak or am interviewed about the secrets of Wal-Mart's success, I begin with our values. I have had many people suggest that all this talk about values sounds more like a simple bromide—mom, apple pie, and baseball. Our values and beliefs are simple—no question about that—but Wal-Mart people understand what they mean and work hard at making them a reality every day. It's not just what's written in the handbook or posted on the walls: Our values must be lived out on every level of our lives and companies.

I've come to realize that beliefs and values together determine how a company operates and whether it reaches its full potential. It works the same on a professional and individual level. Will I lie to a customer or ask someone who works for me to do something unethical? That depends on whether I value people over success. Will I fudge a little on my taxes? That depends on my beliefs about why a person should do the right thing. Will I flirt around just a little as long as it's harmless? That depends on how much I value fidelity in marriage.

Values matter, in everything we do. What do your values look like in everyday life? At home? The workplace?

Blessed is the man

Who walks not in the counsel of the ungodly,

Nor stands in the path of sinners,

Nor sits in the seat of the scornful;

But his delight is in the law of the Lord,

And in His law he meditates day and night.

PSALM 1:1-2

Lead to Make a Difference by...

Spending Time with People

Sam liked the concept of MBWA—"management by walking around." But by his actions he added the letter L to come up with MBWAL— "management by walking around and listening."

THE AUTHOR

My good friend Andy Wilson was the youngest regional vice president in 1987. Only a few months after Andy moved in to the corporate office, the chairman, Sam Walton, stopped by unexpectedly.

Andy quickly rose and shook Sam's hand. Then Sam edged past Andy toward the chair behind his desk. Andy stepped aside, puzzled. Sam said, "Andy, I want to tell you something and I don't want you to forget it." Sam patted the back of the now-empty chair.

"Never make a crucial decision sitting in this chair."

Andy nodded respectfully and scribbled down the phrase. He didn't quite understand the advice, but if it came from Sam, he was sure it meant something important.

Sitting at his desk just a few weeks later, Andy received a call from Rob, a veteran district manager, to let Andy know he would be demoting or firing a store manager. The store was underperforming and a change was needed. Andy was about to agree—when he glanced down at his yellow pad of paper and saw the challenge from Sam written there: *Never make a crucial decision sitting in this chair.*

"Hold on, I'll fly out on Monday," Andy said. "Don't do anything yet. I do not know this manager personally and I have never been to this market."

On Monday morning, Rob picked Andy up from the airport. On their drive to the store, Andy countered Rob's readiness to replace the manager by saying that he liked to talk with the associates before firing anyone. So when they arrived, Andy walked around the store, asking associates about the manager. It didn't take long to find out that he was indeed struggling in his job—but also struggling to care for his wife, who was ill with cancer, and their two children. He was overwhelmed.

Andy went to the front of the store and called Rob over the intercom. When Rob walked up, he asked Andy, "So, are we going to take care of him now?"

"No, we're going for a drive."

In the car, Andy asked, "What's the manager's wife's name?"

Rob didn't know.

"Any ideas on why he's struggling?"

Rob didn't have any.

"How many times do you stop by this store each week?"

Andy quickly related what he had learned and

said, "Because I have the responsibility and the authority to make the right decision, we can do one of two things right now: I can fire you, or we can go back to that store and make this situation right. We are not going to fire this man just because he's going through a hard time." Rob quickly opted for the second choice.

Once there, Andy called all of the associates together and brought the store manager to the front. He addressed the workers: "We need you to rally around him. We're going to give him as much time as he needs to be with his wife and family. In the meantime, there will be an interim manager, but we ask that you all pitch in and give a little more to help this store thrive."

Ultimately, the store manager's wife returned to good health, and he was able to return to his store manager position, where he is very effective today. Andy passed on Sam's lesson about not making decisions from behind a desk. This became a defining moment in Andy's life on leadership. The two men ended up with a lot of mutual respect and a great relationship.

Why? Andy got out from behind his desk and went to where the people were.

> *And when Jesus went out He saw a great*
> *multitude; and He was moved with*
> *compassion for them, and healed their sick.*
>
> MATTHEW 14:14

Lead to Make a Difference by ...

Acting with Integrity

Character is doing the right thing when nobody's looking. There are too many people who think that the only thing that's right is to get by, and the only thing that's wrong is to get caught.

J.C. WATTS

An ethical leader demonstrates integrity and character by his or her actions and by his or her words. When you watch and listen to him or her, they make you feel like you want to be better yourself. Have you had a leader like that in your life? Maybe a parent or teacher or community volunteer? Have you been that kind of leader for others—when they watch and listen to you, they want to do better themselves?

Once, I got an envelope on my desk from an

officer in the company with a note that said, "Use this if you want.   If not, just toss it."   I looked inside and there was a series of profit and loss (P&L) statements for a competitor of ours.   Wow! What a treasure trove.   I've heard rumors that some companies pay a lot of money to get valuable information like this—it's often referred to as corporate espionage.   And here it was on my desk, free of charge.   I would've loved to have peeked—and sure, I was tempted—but I tossed the report in the trash.   It wasn't my property and it was company confidential information that was not for our eyes.

As I think back on that moment, however, I realize I failed.   Why?   Because I didn't study a competitor's numbers?   No!   I failed the person who sent it to me. He passed confidential information that belonged to someone else on to me to make a value judgment.   I clearly knew that studying that report was wrong.   But I never explained to him why it was legally and morally

wrong, and I never let him know what I did with it.
He may still assume I studied their numbers.

On two other occasions, I've had P&Ls of competitors given to me. The first time, one of our regional vice presidents came to me and said, "Don, look what I found. A stack of all their monthly and annual performance reports!"

I explained, "We can't read those." I called the president of the company, a friend of mine, told him I'd put it in the mail, and assured him that his company's papers would not be copied or read. He thanked me profusely. I felt I'd done much better than the first time. I explained to the regional vice president that found them why we couldn't look at them. But I still made a mistake. There was one other thing I could've done better. I could have had the regional vice president talk to the competitor himself.

The next time a P&L was turned over to me, I had the man who found it call the president of the company and send it back. I think that had much greater impact on the individual than if I just took care of it myself. The lesson of doing the right thing was much stronger because he was the one who did it!

A bottom line principle of business—and life—is, do what is right, even when no one else is looking. A leadership corollary is to create an environment through your words and actions where others are motivated to do right as well.

> *Continue to have faith and do what you know is right. Some people have rejected this, and their faith has been shipwrecked.*
>
> 1 TIMOTHY 1:19   NCV

Lead to Make a Difference by ...

Sharing a Vision

Dream lofty dreams, and as you dream, so shall you become.
Your vision is the promise of what you shall one day be;
your ideal is the prophecy of what you shall at last unveil.

JAMES LANE ALLEN

When he looked into the future, Sam didn't see Wal-Mart as the largest retailer in the world. He simply wanted to provide a better shopping experience for everyday people living in small towns. He wanted to improve their standard of living by providing quality goods at low prices in a pleasant shopping environment. He wanted to accomplish this with a team of people who would embrace this same vision, and who were pleasant, hardworking, and dedicated. (Sam checked a person's smile before he checked their educational background when he made his hiring decisions!)   He strongly believed that if his team of associates felt like they were part of a family, it would make his vision a joy and a success.   And ultimately, as a smart businessman, Sam realized that if the stores were successful, he could continue to grow the company and touch more customers with his vision.

Notice that Sam did not begin with a vision to create the largest retail chain in the United States—much less found the largest company in the world.   Millions of people have ambitious dreams and grand ideas for the future, but fail to build the support and enthusiasm of others—investors, customers, their own employees. Maybe even themselves. If you want people to follow you, be aware that they will always relate much better and on a much deeper level to something that is worthwhile in and of itself rather than financial objectives.   Sam adopted a simple business plan that was fueled by a belief that it would likewise make the world a better place.

Did he really believe his retail model would change the world? Yes, he did. Passionately. And that was one of the key reasons his team embraced the vision.

The customers bought into the vision, too. They continued to shop at Wal-Mart, making the vision a reality—and helping it to grow beyond anything Sam ever dreamed of. Sam never wavered in his vision to provide service to small town America. The vision grew, but the fundamental premise never changed— improve the standard of living for everyday people by providing quality goods at low prices.

What's your vision for your life? For your family? For your company? Does it inspire others? Does it inspire you?

> *Where there is no vision, the people perish:*
> *but he that keepeth the law, happy is he.*
>
> PROVERBS 29:18 KJV

Lead to Make a Difference by...

Building Trust

Trust is the emotional glue that
binds followers and leaders together.

WARREN BENNIS

Trust is the foundation of all life's relationships. It is an essential ingredient in successful leadership. It is not something that we are entitled to—it must be earned.

When an individual is promoted or a new leader joins an organization, regardless of their reputation, they must prove themselves. Certainly they must prove that they are technically competent—but perhaps most of all, everyone is watching how that individual treats people. Do they genuinely care about others? Do they demonstrate a measure of humility, or do they have a big ego? Are they someone who listens to the opinions of others, or do they feel they have all the answers. Is this a person of integrity—can we really trust them?

The way a new leader acts will demonstrate to everyone in the organization what kind of person they are. Everyone will develop their own perception, which will likely last a long time. That perception will, in large measure, determine how the people respond.

I've only worked for three companies in my career, and when I joined each one I had to prove myself all over again. When I started with Wal-Mart, I came in as an executive vice president. I'm sure there were others in the organization that wondered why Sam went outside the company and didn't promote them. I felt like I was under a microscope. They watched everything I did. I was tested numerous times to see how I would react. It took a while before I began to feel like people really trusted me, and it was only then I could really accomplish everything that I was brought into the company to do. You see, it didn't matter that Sam trusted me—the people

I worked with had to develop their own trust. If I had disappointed or failed them, it wouldn't have worked.

It was up to me to demonstrate who I really was; it wasn't up to the people. I had to earn their respect.

What would have happened if I had done something inappropriate? What if I lied to any one of them, or didn't keep a promise, or mistreated them? I would have breached our trust relationship. Once trust is broken, it takes a long time to restore—and in some cases, trust is never regained. Unfortunately, I saw that happen to several individuals during my career. How sad!

Trust is a precious commodity in all of our relationships. Remember, many people are watching you and counting on you. Be trustworthy.

> *Many people claim to be loyal, but it is hard to find a trustworthy person.*
>
> PROVERBS 20:6 NCV

Lead to Make a Difference by...

Acting Decisively

*Thinking is easy, action is difficult. To act in accordance
with one's thought is the most difficult thing in the world.*

GOETHE

To be a great leader, you must have the ability to
think, to reflect, to involve others in decisions, to listen
and communicate effectively, and to build consensus.
But you also have to be able to act.

It is the same way in our walk of faith. One anonymous
poet said it like this:

*I was hungry
    and you formed a debate team
    to debate the pros and cons
    of world hunger relief.*

I was imprisoned

   and you crept away busily

   hoping someone would

   somehow find time to visit me.

I was poorly clothed

   and in your mind you disapproved

   of my lack of style.

I was sick

   and you thanked God

   for your good health.

I was homeless

   and you preached about the spiritual shelter of the church.

I was lonely

   and you muttered a quick prayer

   and left me alone.

You seem so content

   so pleased with your Christianity

   but I'm still hungry and

   lonely and cold.

One of my favorite Bible stories is of Nehemiah. God gave him the job of leading the Jewish exiles back to their homeland and rebuilding the walls of the city of Jerusalem after a seventy-year period when the city had fallen into neglect and ruin. A number of local political leaders didn't want to see this happen. Perhaps the most powerful, a man named Sanballat, approached Nehemiah as he began construction and suggested, "Let's meet together and pray."

Nehemiah's answer was classic. Your Bible may not say it quite this way, but my paraphrase is simple and to-the-point: "We've already prayed. It's time to roll up our sleeves and build the wall."

One of the greatest things Sam Walton taught me is that a leader stays involved in his business and close to his people so that he can quickly determine the best course of action—and then act. We constantly monitored our profits and losses, visited stores, and talked to associates to find out what was really going on. We always had plenty of information, so we didn't need to hold three days' worth of meetings to figure out what to do next. We made plans for improvement quickly, and then executed those plans immediately. As an example, decisions made in Friday meetings, were implemented in stores by Monday morning.

After appropriate discussion and reflection, today's great leader will act decisively.

> *In the same way, faith that is alone—*
> *that does nothing—is dead.*
>
> JAMES 2:17 NCV

Lead to Make a Difference by...

Serving Others

We need authentic leaders who are committed
to stewardship of their assets and to making
a difference in the lives of the people they serve.

BILL GEORGE, FORMER CEO, MEDTRONICS

In his classic little novel, *Journey to the East,* Herman Hesse spins a tale of a band of rich and powerful men who have been recruited for an adventure that promises them great wealth and glory. None of the men know the name of the mysterious man who put the pilgrimage together, nor even the final destination of their journey. Their only information comes through a humble servant, Leo, who prepares their food, polishes their boots, and plays the guitar and sings to them each night as they fall to sleep.

After a time, the journey is unpleasant and increasingly difficult as these powerful men jockey for position and bicker among themselves on who should be the leader and make decisions. And when their servant Leo disappears one night, things take an even more dramatic turn for the worse. One by one, the men desert the party and return home broken by this grand failure. One man determines that he will find the mysterious sponsor of the scheme to find out where they went wrong. It takes him years, but he finally tracks this shadowy and mysterious character down, only to discover that it was Leo. Leo points out that as long as the group had a servant, they had a leader; when they lost their servant, they lost their leader.

Leo reminds him what he already knew in his heart: Great tasks require great servants.

Do leaders today really serve? There are a lot of references to "servant leadership" flying around corporate discussions, but my observation is that few people really seem to understand it or practice it. I see a lot of top leaders who seem much more interested in their own compensation, comfort, and welfare than they do about their associates, their product, and their customers.

Jesus Christ, the greatest leader to ever walk the earth, was a wonderful example of servant leadership in every aspect of His life. He ministered to the poor (Luke 4:18); He gave up all the comforts of house and home to do the will of His Father (Matthew 8:20); He made the ultimate sacrifice by laying down His life for the sins of the world (John 10:15).

In the great room in our training facility for the Soderquist Center for Ethical Leadership, we have a beautiful bronze statue of Christ washing a disciple's feet. It serves as a constant reminder to us of how we should lead: serving others.

True servant leaders:

- Believe in and feel responsibility for the growth and development of their people.

- Share not only the responsibility but also the recognition for success.

- Don't ask others to do what they aren't willing to do themselves—there are no tasks "beneath" them.

- Establish relationships built on mutual respect and trust—and not just among top executives but at every level of their companies.

- Care about and look for ways to meet the needs of everyone they come in contact with, including associates, suppliers, and customers.

How do the people who work for you view you? Egotistical? Self-serving? Or do others want to serve you because of the way you serve them?

> *A disciple is not above his teacher,*
> *nor a servant above his master.*
>
> MATTHEW 10:24

Lead to Make a Difference by ...

Overcoming Adversity

*We shall draw from the heart of suffering
itself the means of inspiration and survival.*

WINSTON CHURCHILL

Gary was diagnosed with cancer at the age of sixty-four. Over the next thirteen months, he lost seventy pounds and endured treatments and surgeries—but came out cancer free. How'd he handle it? He bought a bike. He declared himself a "Lance Armstrong wannabe" and determined that if Lance Armstrong could beat cancer and win the Tour de France, he could achieve great things after his cancer recovery, too. In the end, Gary became stronger and healthier than he was before his cancer diagnosis.

We can live, learn, and lead to the best of our abilities, with the highest standards of integrity—and still get knocked flat on our faces. Our best plans, intentions, and prayers can't (and don't) ensure a trouble free life.

I might even go so far as to say that all great accomplishments will be accompanied by pain.

We understand the concept of "no pain, no gain" when we're working out at the gym. But it's a whole other story when we—or someone we love—faces unavoidable physical or emotional pain.

Does God hurt us in order to make us stronger? The Bible says that God doesn't tempt us (James 1:13), but He does allow trials to enter into our lives. The Bible also says we should "hold on" during our sufferings "because they are like a father's discipline" (Hebrews 12:7 NCV).

The writer of the book of Hebrews also calls for his persecuted flock of Christians not to "get tired and stop trying" (12:3 NCV). He reminds them that in tough times, if we want to win the race, we must get rid of things that hinder us and sin that entangles us. We can't run with extra weight and cords around our ankles. But even more importantly, he calls all of us to keep our eyes on Jesus, the author and perfector of our faith, who showed us how to run the race of life with perseverance (12:4). When we see our final destination and know that others have gone before us, it makes even the difficult moments of the journey more than bearable.

Here are a few reminders to bolster your soul when you experience pain in your life—

- God will not allow anything to happen to you that you cannot bear (1 Corinthians 10:13).
- God is able to transform painful experiences into profound and powerful life lessons (Romans 8:28).
- God uses those who have experienced pain to bring comfort to others who are hurting today (2 Corinthians 1:4).

God wants only what's best for us—but He knows that sometimes the only road to character is through pain.   The good news is that Jesus runs beside us each step of the way.

My brethren, count it all joy when you fall into various trials, knowing that the testing of your faith produces patience. But let patience have its perfect work, that you may be perfect and complete, lacking nothing.

JAMES 1:2-4

Lead to Make a Difference by...

Trusting God

Walk boldly and wisely.   There is a
hand above that will help you on.

PHILIP JAMES BAILEY

I joined Wal-Mart in April 1980.   At the time, the company's annual sales were $1.2 billion.   When I retired from the Board of Directors twenty-two years later, the company's sales were $244 billion that year, and we were the largest company in the world.   What an adventure!

I went to work for Wal-Mart after having served as the president of a significant national retailer.   I already had strong feelings of awe and humility with where my career had taken me.   I didn't enter the work world with any preconceived notions of carving out a huge business career for myself. Sure, I was ambitious and wanted to do well, but matters of faith and family were more important to me. That's how I'd been raised.

I've penned this book not from the perspective of a powerful mover and shaker who has all the answers—because I don't—but as someone who holds the simple belief that if you live your life in the right way and with the right values, God will take care of the rest. God's plans will always be better than the ones we come up with ourselves. I'm a living testament to that!

I've made my share of mistakes along the way, and I know for a fact that it wasn't my wisdom and business skills that brought me success. I can truly say that I'm a blessed individual—and one of my great blessings was working side by side with a man named Sam Walton. He truly knew how to live, learn, and lead. He was generous to pass on what he believed and what he knew to thousands of others. I wrote this book hoping that as you read these short reflections from my personal life and thoughts, my relationship with Sam and countless other cherished colleagues, and my career at Wal-Mart, you would be inspired to live, learn, and lead to the fullest.

But true success won't come by reading a book or following a list of principles, however wise and good they might be. Sure, those things might help and provide a nudge in the right direction, but what really matters most is your relationship with God. If you hear and heed nothing else in this book, what I hope and pray you take with you is a renewed sense of trust in the plans and purposes of a loving God for *your* life as you live, learn, and lead.

> *Trust in the Lord with all your heart,*
> *And lean not on your own understanding;*
> *In all your ways acknowledge Him,*
> *And He shall direct your paths.*
>
> PROVERBS 3:5-6

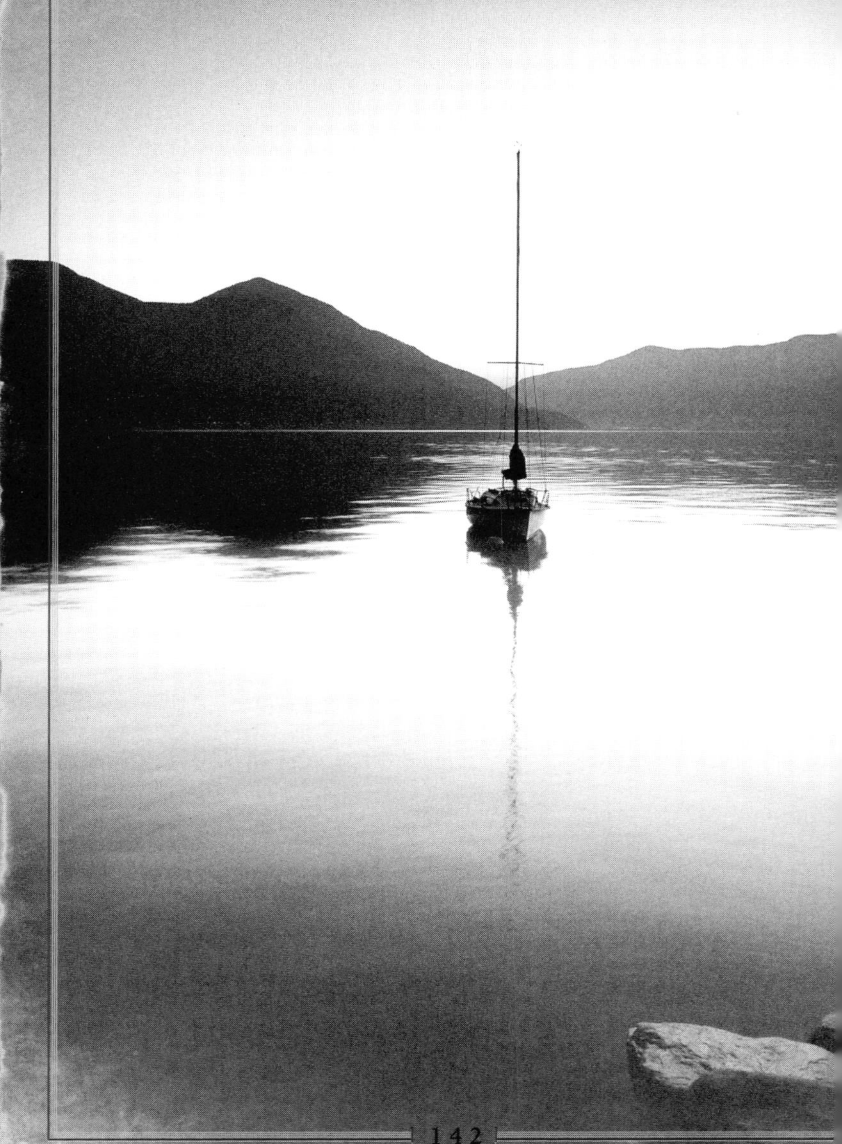

Prayer for Living

Dear Heavenly Father,

Thank You that You meet me where I am today.   You know my needs.   You care about me.   You are good and kind.

Lord, help me live according to Your purposes.   Create in me a clean heart, O God—may my day-to-day actions and interactions reflect You.   Protect me from temptation.   Help me to bless those around me.

Lord, make me willing and able to learn every day.   Show me the truths You want me to know.   Give me the humility to correct mistakes and realign my thinking according to Your Word.

Lord, I'm in awe of the responsibility I have to lead—and follow—others.   Help me shepherd the people in my care with patience, love, and wisdom.   Help me to follow the leaders in my life with loyalty and insight.   Strengthen me, Lord God, and guide my every decision.

In Jesus' name I pray, Amen.

About the Author

Don Soderquist, retired Senior Vice Chairman of the board for Wal-Mart Stores, Inc., spent over twenty years with Wal-Mart.   After Sam Walton died, Don became known throughout the company as the "Keeper of the Culture."

Don led the company as Chief Operating Officer during a period marked by exponential growth.

Wal-Mart's success is grounded in the highly ethical, performance-focused, servant leadership philosophies of Sam and Don continued to work hard to instill them in the heart of every associate.

For the past four years Don has dedicated his energies to establishing a non-profit organization, the Soderquist Center for Leadership and Ethics, which is affiliated with the John Brown University and its school of business. He conducts seminars for executives and managers of many Fortune 500 companies, as well as companies of all size.   He is a much

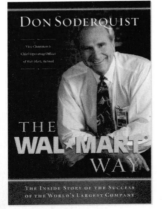

sought after motivational speaker.

He and his wife, Jo, have four children and ten grandchildren, and live in Rogers, Arkansas, along with his dog, Charlie.

VISIT WWW.SODERQUIST.ORG
FOR MORE INFORMATION ABOUT THE
CENTER FOR LEADERSHIP AND ETHICS
AND TO VIEW DON'S BOOK,
The Wal-Mart Way (NELSON BOOKS 2005)
GO TO WWW.THOMASNELSON.COM AND
CLICK ON NELSON BOOKS.